CREATIVE LIVES

Willy Russell

SHAUN McCARTHY

www.heinemann.co.uk/library
Visit our website to find out more information about **Heinemann Library** books.

To order:
☎ Phone 44 (0) 1865 888066
📄 Send a fax to 44 (0) 1865 314091
💻 Visit the Heinemann Bookshop at www.heinemann.co.uk/library to browse our catalogue and order online.

First published in Great Britain by Heinemann Library, Halley Court, Jordan Hill, Oxford OX2 8EJ, a division of Reed Educational and Professional Publishing Ltd. Heinemann is a registered trademark of Reed Educational and Professional Publishing Ltd.

OXFORD MELBOURNE AUCKLAND JOHANNESBURG BLANTYRE
GABORONE IBADAN PORTSMOUTH NH (USA) CHICAGO

Designed by Tinstar Design (www.tinstar.co.uk)
Originated by Ambassador Litho Ltd
Printed and bound by South China Printing Company Ltd in Hong Kong/China

ISBN 0 431 13998 9
06 05 04 03 02
10 9 8 7 6 5 4 3 2 1

British Library Cataloguing in Publication Data
McCarthy, Shaun
      Willy Russell. – (Creative Lives)
      1. Russell, Willy
      2. Dramatists, English – 20th century – Biography – Juvenile literature
      I.Title
      822.9'14

Acknowledgements
The Publishers would like to thank the following for permission to reproduce photographs:
Advertising Archives: p46; BBC Photograph Library: pp28, 34; Catherine Ashmore: p32; Charles Negus-Fancey: p51; Corbis: pp4, 8; Hulton Archive: pp11, 12, 19; Liverpool Central Records Office: pp24, 31, 33; Liverpool Echo: pp6, 9, 21, 25, 39; PA Photos: p55; Photostage/Donald Cooper: pp5, 26, 37, 43; Popperfoto: p22; Redferns/Max Scheler: p17; Robbie Jack Photography: pp48, 49; Robert Harding Picture Library: p27; Ronald Grant Archive: pp45, 53; St Helens Local History & Archives Library: p14; Universal Pictorial Press & Agency: p41.

Cover photograph reproduced with permission of Corbis.

Picture research by Kay Altwegg.

The author and Publishers would like to thank Willy Russell for his invaluable help in writing this book.

Thanks also to Methuen Publishing Limited for permission to reproduce notes and extracts from Willy Russell's *Our Day Out*, *One for the Road*, *Stags and Hens* and *Educating Rita*.

Contents

Any words appearing in the text in bold, **like this**, are explained in the Glossary.

Voice of the ordinary people

Willy Russell is one of the most successful **playwrights** in the world today. He has written many hit shows for the stage, including the award-winning musical *Blood Brothers*. Two of his most popular stage plays, *Educating Rita* and *Shirley Valentine*, have been made into successful, prize-winning films. He has also written dramas for television and radio. Unlike many writers, he writes his own lyrics to the songs in his musicals, and even composed the music for *Blood Brothers*. He **adapts** his stage shows himself when they are turned into films. But although he has accepted new challenges throughout his career, and has always written something hugely successful in each new form, there has always been a clear, consistent focus at the heart of his writing.

Willy Russell in his home city of Liverpool. The city and its people have been the inspiration for almost all of his plays and film scripts.

A scene from a 1988 London theatre production of *Blood Brothers*, Willy Russell's hugely successful musical.

Willy Russell is famous for writing about his hometown, Liverpool, and the 'ordinary' people living there. He writes about **working-class** people, and especially working-class women who struggle to change lives that threaten to restrict and limit them. He has never written a play set in another time, or in a different country. He writes for the most part about the city where he has always lived and about the sort of people he went to school with.

'Up in lights'

His careers teacher thought that all boys from Willy Russell's sort of background who did not do well at school would go and work at the local bottle factory. When Willy Russell left school he became a ladies' hairdresser instead! Many of his classmates believed (like the young men and women in his play *Stags and Hens*) that you'd get married young, have kids, live on an estate near your parents, and that would be that! Today, Willy Russell's name has literally been 'up in lights' outside theatres in London, New York and other major cities around the world. He has made a career from writing stories, plays, songs and recently, a novel. It is a way of life a million miles away from the one he once thought would be his. How did he do it?

Early days

William Martin Russell was born in 1947 at Whiston Hospital. Whiston is a small town between the city of Liverpool and the industrial town of St Helens, in north-west England. The Russell family lived in nearby Rainhill, which was famous locally for its large **mental asylum**. According to Willy Russell, 'Any admission of coming from Rainhill would provoke [from other kids] mockery and accusations of lunacy, so I learnt from an early age to claim Whiston as my true birthplace.'

When Willy Russell was born, World War II had ended only two years earlier. The Russells lived on an estate of 300 houses that had been built to house **munitions** workers during the war. It was a **working-class** community. Although Willy Russell has a sister, Dawn, she is seventeen years younger than him, so he really grew up as an only child.

Although they were working-class people, the Russell family had a tradition of developing small businesses. Willy Russell's grandmother

Dee Road, Rainhill, on the outskirts of Liverpool, where Willy Russell spent the first years of his life.

ran a 'mobile' grocer's shop near his first school: 'It was in an old **charabanc** which long since lost any chance of going anywhere, but everyone called it the mobile.'

Perhaps following this family tradition of enterprise, Willy Russell's father left his factory job and ended up running a chip shop. He had been a miner and had worked in a metals factory. He was not directly involved in politics but felt passionately about them. According to Willy Russell, 'He was not a party member or a tub-thumping **Socialist** but he was very firmly on the side of the **underdog**... He liked nothing better on a Saturday night than to have a heated discussion with three or four people on politics or religion.'

His father admitted that he had not learnt much at school. When he was eighteen he went to night school to try to catch up on some of the education he had missed (very much like his son would do many years later). But Willy Russell's father had an interest in books and reading. At one time he bought a selection of books, packed them into two cases mounted on the back of a bicycle, and toured the neighbourhood running his own mobile lending library!

Willy Russell was also influenced by his mother, who inspired her son with different values. 'She had great natural sympathy, and **aspirations**. She liked nice things, delicate things which my father distrusted. She realised that refinement and taste had nothing to do with class, whereas my father thought they were posh or **bourgeois**.'

Influence and inspiration

Female relatives were a big part of Willy Russell's early life. Apart from his grandmother with her immobile 'mobile' shop, there were aunts living nearby on the same estate. The men worked long hours on shifts in local factories so Willy Russell often found himself in a house full of women. He was not old enough to go to school, and he remembers that, 'When you are a toddler women tend to be unguarded. They will talk about things they don't think a four-year-old will take in... so it may be that the women's view of the world seeped into my pores from a very early age.'

'[My parents were] *passionately opposed to mob culture or mob thought. They could never stand unquestioning groups of people and I was brought up to see both sides of a question.*'
Willy Russell, on the influence of his parents.

A father who was passionate about equality and justice. A mother with a love for the more refined things in life that society at the time thought were beyond working-class people. And a house full of women behaving as if the young Willy Russell was not there. All these family influences would inspire his writing in the years to come.

Liverpool and its people

Liverpool always had **slums** and poor areas, and the city suffered heavy bomb damage from German Luftwaffe (air force) attacks on the city's docks along the River Mersey. Whiston was not part of this inner-city world, but Willy Russell would have been aware of the hard lives and poor living conditions many people in Liverpool endured, not least through the tales of his mother, who had grown up in the city.

When Willy Russell was five his family moved to Knowsley. This was closer to the centre of Liverpool and had a stronger connection to the city than Whiston. The Russells moved onto an estate full of working-class people who had lived in the city centre. After the war, most working-class men in Liverpool worked for big industrial firms. Apart from the docks and shipyards, the city had many factories, including Ford Cars at Halewood, and the glass and bottle factories at St Helens.

A mother with her young child in the slums of Liverpool in 1957. Many people of Willy Russell's generation grew up in poverty in areas like this.

A view of the famous River Mersey waterfront at Liverpool, which is visited by thousands of tourists every year. The office building with the two tall towers is the Liver Building. At the top of each tower is a big carving of a **mythical** bird, together known as the 'Liver Birds'.

Willy Russell has lived in or near the city all his life and has seen many of these great industries close and tens of thousands of men lose their jobs. He has seen the lives and the identity of so-called working-class people change dramatically. Some of these social changes are reflected in his plays. But he is primarily interested in writing about individuals – characters with powerful and moving stories to tell.

'Scousers'

Liverpool has always had a strong sense of its own unique identity. Its people – nicknamed 'Scousers' – are famed for their sense of humour. Their accent, made famous by the Beatles and other Liverpool-born entertainers, is something they are proud of. Even people from just outside the city are thought by **Liverpudlians** to have a different way of speaking, even people from places as close as Whiston or Rainhill! Willy Russell said of his childhood: 'They talk funny in Whiston. To a Liverpudlian everyone else talks funny. Fortunately, when I was five my mum and dad moved to Knowsley, into an area full of Liverpudlians who taught me how to talk correctly.' He soon acquired his Liverpool accent.

Schools good and bad

Inspired by his own experiences, several of Willy Russell's plays deal with childhood, school days and education. His 1977 television play *Our Day Out* (which was later **adapted** for stage) and *Blood Brothers*, his enormously successful stage musical, both deal with the issue of young people growing up.

Willy Russell's first school was in Knowsley. He learnt to read at a very young age, but apart from reading books and playing football, he remembers only really enjoying the twice-weekly gardening lessons, where pupils learnt to grow vegetables on little plots in the school grounds. When he has been interviewed about his childhood and school days he has painted extremely vivid pictures of people and events, as if they were still a part of his life. He has used one of the great skills that a successful **playwright** needs – the ability to think and write in character.

Surviving Huyton

Then came a terrible shock. When he was eleven years old, Willy Russell had to move up to secondary school. This was a much bigger school in nearby Huyton, another edge-of-the-city suburb, but set in the middle of a huge housing estate. The little world of the school at Knowsley was blown away forever. 'Everyone said there were gangs (in Huyton) with bike chains and broken bottles and truck spanners. What they said was right: playtime was nothing to do with play, it was about survival.'

'Pop Chandler's leg'

In one interview Willy Russell fondly remembers the head teacher of his first school in Knowsley. Although it is the grown-up Willy Russell speaking, some 30 years later, it sounds like a young boy recounting what has happened in school. 'Pop Chandler had a war wound in his leg. Everyone said it was 'cos of the **shrapnel**. When we went to the swimming baths (if he was in a good mood) he'd show us this hole in his leg. It was horrible. It was blue. We loved looking at it.'

Willy Russell describes himself as being 'quite tough' at school. He enjoyed sport, especially football, but stopped playing because, as he puts it, 'I began to discover cigarettes, girls and guitars.' (Today, many years later, he plays tennis and describes himself as a 'closet Evertonian' – that is, a secret supporter of Everton, one of Liverpool's two great football teams.)

He remembers being shocked by the way some other pupils behaved. More frightening though were some of the teachers. When he talks about his school days, he **glosses over** the memories with his trademark dry humour, but there is no doubt he felt a terrifying sense that the school was mapping out a future for him – a future he did not want. Most boys from schools like the one at Huyton went straight into **manual jobs** in local factories. They were nicknamed 'factory fodder', an expression Willy Russell would come to hate.

A lunch-time game of football in a school in the early 1960s. In his writing about childhood, Willy Russell brings to life scenes like this, which could be both fun and frightening.

Silent reading

Willy Russell was not very good at practical school subjects. Woodwork and metalwork were taught to boys that the school expected would go to work in the **trades**, and to manual jobs in factories. His metalwork teacher made him do his first simple piece of work over and over again for a whole year. Remembering this, Willy Russell said: 'It's the only time I can remember feeling real hatred for another human being.' For a man who usually displays much good humour, this shows the depth of despair he felt about his new school. What he did not know then was that his experiences were setting the foundations for some of the most powerful characters in his plays: the **working-class** individuals who struggle against 'the system' to change their lives.

Woodwork and metalwork classes in the 1960s taught boys the practical skills they would need to get a factory job.

> " "
> 'First thing we had to do was file a small rectangle of metal so that all the sides were straight, this would then be used as a name tag to identify each kid's work. I never completed mine. Other kids moved on producing guns, daggers and boiler room engines while it was obvious that I was never going to be able to get the side of my piece of metal straight. Eventually it was just a sliver, like a needle, though not straight. I showed it (to the teacher). He chucked it in the bin and wordlessly handed me another chunk of metal and indicated that I had to do it again and again and again until I did it right! For a whole year, every metalwork lesson, I tried and failed and with every failure there came a chunk of metal and instructions to do it again.'
>
> Willy Russell, on the trials and tribulations of school metalwork lessons

He began to have nightmares about metalwork lessons. But things suddenly got better. After a year in Huyton he moved schools, to Rainford, still nearby but further out in the country between Liverpool and St Helens, 'where there were fields and lawns instead of concrete playgrounds, and compared to Huyton it was paradise'. His usual tone of good humour returns when he remembers Rainford: 'The thugs were old-fashioned, charming even… You could still get hurt of course, and some of the teachers were headcases; but there were no sadists, and metalwork was not on the curriculum.'

But silent reading was on the curriculum. The school timetable had a lesson in which you just picked up a book, settled down and, provided you stayed quiet, just read on as long as you wanted. Russell loved these silent reading lessons. It was during one of them, 'locked into a novel, the sun streaming through the windows, experiencing the feeling of total peace and security', that he had a sudden startling idea – he wanted to be a writer!

That feeling of being young, wanting something badly but not knowing how to get it was used by Willy Russell in his television play for schools *The Boy With The Transistor Radio*. The main character, Terry, listens to a radio DJ constantly telling listeners how good everything is going to be. But Terry's life isn't going anywhere. With his young life falling apart at the end of the play, he ends up trying to learn to play a guitar. His efforts are 'painful but determined'. He may make it. Willy Russell did.

The bottle factory

Russell was fourteen years old, and happily thinking what a great occupation it would be to write books. He wanted to bring to others the same sort of pleasure that reading brought to him. But there was a problem. Even at Rainford, boys like Willy Russell were still considered 'factory fodder'. He was in the D stream, close to the bottom of the grades at school, and had not worked hard at any of the subjects he

A typical factory scene from the 1950s. Willy Russell dreaded the thought of spending his working life in a place like this.

would take exams in. His wish to be a writer was sudden, strong and thrilling. But he felt he had to hide it. He felt he would have to become a completely different person to write books, because people like him, from backgrounds like his, never did anything like writing books. So he hid his precious idea. But it did not go away.

During his last year at school, Willy Russell and the other pupils who were not thought likely to pass many exams, were taken on a trip to a huge bottle-making factory nearby. He was filled with horror, and paints a vivid picture of the effect the visit had on him:

'I could feel the brutality of the place even before I entered its windowless walls. Inside, the din and the smell were overpowering. Human beings worked in there but the figures I saw, feeding huge and relentlessly hungry machines, seemed not to be part of humanity but part of the machinery itself... Most of the kids with whom I visited the place accepted that it was their lot to end up there. Some even talked of the money they would earn and made out that they couldn't wait to get inside those walls... But I think they all dreaded it as much as I.'

This is a powerful description of the shock of the scene. But notice that while many writers might be **disdainful** of the other boys who said they were happy to go into the factory, Willy Russell is compassionate. He saw, or at least imagined, their fear of what the future held. He was shocked by the system, not angry with the people who had to live within it. This ability to understand and sympathize with ordinary people, and the lives they have to live, has been a major influence in the characters he has created in his plays. And the options that life gives young people, according to what sort of background or class they were born into, is a powerful theme in *Blood Brothers*.

In this musical, a poor and struggling mother gives away one of her new-born twins to a much better off middle-class woman who cannot have children. The son that stays with his real mother has a completely different life from his brother. The differences – the schools they attend, the friends thay have in the streets where they live, etc – are all created by money and the **class system**.

Hairdressing

After the visit to the bottle factory, Willy Russell went to school determined to try and alter the awful future that he felt was waiting for him. But he realized he had left it all too late! There were just six months to go before final exams. He felt **disheartened** by the schoolwork he could not hope to get done. Instead of studying he started going to listen to lunchtime music sessions in a cellar music club in the middle of Liverpool. The little Cavern Club was soon to become world famous. It was the place where a new group first appeared – The Beatles.

At school Willy Russell was part of a group of boys who felt they did not belong to any of the main social groups. They wanted things in the future that were supposed to be beyond the expectations of 'normal' **working-class** boys. They could have become bullied outsiders, but because they were good at sports they were not picked on by the others. In the summer of 1962 Willy Russell left school with just one O level, in English Language. He had also learnt to play the guitar. What was he going to do now?

The Beatles

Considered by many people to be the most popular and influential pop group ever, The Beatles were formed in Liverpool in 1960 by John Lennon, Paul McCartney, George Harrison and Ringo Starr. Soon after their first appearance at the Cavern Club in Liverpool and elsewhere in the UK, the halls overflowed with idolizing fans. 'Beatlemania' spread around the world in the next few years, **buoyed** by international hits such as 'She Loves You' and 'I Want to Hold Your Hand', and by the overwhelming success of a huge tour in American stadiums. Other early hits, all written by Lennon and McCartney, included 'Please Please Me', 'Can't Buy Me Love', 'And I Love Her', and 'Yesterday'. In 1966 the Beatles stopped performing in public. The group split up in 1970, and each member pursued a solo career. Apart from perhaps John Lennon, none of them ever gained the same level of fame for their music that they had enjoyed as The Beatles.

One day he went straight from listening to a group at a lunchtime session in the Cavern Club to sit an examination to become an **apprentice** printer. This was his father's idea. Printers could earn good money. Printing was a trade, with skills that had to be learnt. A print room was more of a workshop than an enormous factory, even if you did have to learn how to work machines. And to Willy Russell, printing

The Cavern Club in the early 1960s. Willy Russell remembers lunchtimes there: 'The smell of sweat in there was as **pungent** as any in a factory, the din was louder than any made by machines. But the sweat was mingled with cheap perfume and was produced by dancing and the noise was music, made by a group called The Beatles.'

seemed closer to the world of books than bottle-making! For part of the exam he had to write an essay. His was entitled 'A Group Called The Beatles'. He failed the exam.

A wild idea

Willy Russell always says he had a happy childhood with a supportive family, but this new failure was the cause of 'conferences, discussions, rows and **slanging matches**' at home. Suddenly his mother suggested that he could train to become a hairdresser! This was a wild idea: young men in Liverpool from his background generally went into the **trades** or heavy **manual labour**. They did not 'play about' doing women's hair. But for Willy Russell, 'It was such a bizarre suggestion I went along with it.'

In 1962, he started at the Continental School of Hairdressing. For a year, he learnt how to cut hair, do perms and colouring and all the other skills hairdressing required. Perhaps he just wanted another year in some kind of educational environment before having to make a career choice. He admits he never really wanted to be a hairdresser, that he never really wanted to be anything other than a writer – but that would be a more bizarre suggestion than training to cut women's hair. Hairdressing was at least thought of as an 'arty' sort of job. He remembers that his friends thought it was 'all right', and that all their mothers and sisters were keen for him to do their hair!

> "
> *'There were heads scalded during shampooing, heads which should have become blonde but turned out green, heads of Afro frizz (before Afro frizz had been invented) and heads rendered temporarily bald. Somehow, probably from moving from one shop to another before my legendary abilities were known, I survived.'*
> "
>
> Willy Russell remembers his first attempts at hairdressing

'I want to be a writer'

Willy Russell admits that he did not work any harder at hairdressing school than he had at his previous education. He spent a lot of time at the Cavern Club and at parties. With the help of his guitar, he started to write songs and perform them at small folk clubs. He then began playing in a band with two friends. They called themselves the Kirkby Town Three. (Kirkby is an area of Liverpool.)

He was shocked when he left hairdressing school and found an employer ready to let him 'loose on the heads of innocent and unsuspecting customers'. He was a hairdresser from 1963 to 1968, eventually running his own salon. But he had not given up his dream of being a writer.

When he had no customers, he would go into the shop's back room and write songs. He also tried writing poetry and comic sketches. In the

Annie and 'Willy'

Willy Russell met Annie Seagroatt, who was later to become his wife, in 1966, when he was running and singing in a folk café in Liverpool. They married in 1969. She encouraged him to train to be a teacher, as she was doing, and to turn his creative energies towards writing plays. It was also in 1966 that he first became known as 'Willy'. Until then he had always been known as 'Billy' or 'Bill'. One night in the Green Moose folk café a singer who knew him was parodying a song called *Lilly White Lilly*, changing the chorus to *Willy White Willy* – and the name stuck. Willy (as he now was) liked the change.

mid-1960s, Liverpool was at the forefront of popular music and was world famous. This was the 'swinging sixties' – there was a feeling that anyone could be a song writer, a guitarist or a writer. The trouble was, very few people did more than learn a few chords on the guitar, or dream about the book they wanted to write.

Willy Russell realized he couldn't be a serious writer if he had to keep breaking off to do people's hair. He needed a different job, but he had never really thought that writing could be a proper job. Seeing students in the city, enjoying long holidays, he decided that if he became a student he could use the breaks from college to write.

Class betrayal

Doing what was expected of you, what all your friends did, was a very strong drive in working-class people in the 1960s. It forms the plot of

Willy Russell's play *Stags and Hens*. He felt that some people were shocked and hurt when he explained his plan to them: to become a student, then a writer.

He used this idea in his play *Educating Rita*, when Rita's husband Denny accuses her of deserting her family, of betraying her 'people', by trying to get an education. Annie had quite the reverse influence on Willy Russell: she helped him plan a future where he could have time to write.

Willy Russell wrote songs and performed them with his band at small folk clubs like this one.

Finding a voice

The years of hairdressing were not wasted. Willy Russell had picked up the way working-class **Liverpudlian** women spoke from listening to his customers. He went on to use their speech in many of his most famous plays. He is very good at writing female characters who see how working-class life can oppress women, and who try to overcome these prejudices and limits. Linda in *Stags and Hens* runs away the night before her wedding not just to escape her husband (who spends the whole play passed-out drunk with his head down the toilet!) but to avoid the life she sees she will be expected to lead. Rita in *Educating Rita* loses her husband in her fight to gain an education. Mrs Johnson in *Blood Brothers* gives up a son in order to help the rest of her fatherless children. All of these characters speak with strong Liverpudlian voices.

A new challenge

Willy Russell now faced a challenge as daunting as any encountered by the characters in his plays. After successfully taking and passing another O level, in English literature at evening class, he realized he would have to study full-time just to get the O levels needed for entry into higher education.

Upon learning this, Willy Russell stormed round to the Liverpool Education Department offices to make a complaint. He was blocked at the reception desk. He was furious, but on his way out he saw a poster

A second chance?

Willy Russell remembers this time of struggle with bitterness. 'I started the hellish trek to try to get what is nowadays a completely acceptable thing for a working-class person who's missed an education – a return to learning.' But things were different back in 1967. He was turned away from one college after another. One principal said 'Listen son, you failed at school. You did nothing there, you abused the sytem. Why should I help you or give you a second chance?'

Willy Russell says that getting into Childwall College (below) 'Saved my life: I have no hesitation in saying that. I think that on that day, if I hadn't got on a bus and gone out to Childwall, or if I'd come up against another **authoritarian Luddite** I might have crumbled and decided the wall was just too high. It let me go back to the beginning. It gave me the chance to start again.'

in the foyer advertising a college that offered a package of O levels. He jumped on a bus and went dashing into Childwall College.

'I must have been in a terrible state. The deputy head sat me down in his office, calmed me down and asked me what the problem was. It was such a tender thing to do.' After explaining what had happened, the deputy said that if Russell could pass a basic English test the college would take him. Willy Russell said he already had English Language O level. 'You're in,' said the deputy head. 'It was one of the most significant moments of my life.'

The Ford car factory, Halewood, in 1969, where Willy Russell worked nights cleaning oil from the girders high above the assembly lines.

Danger money

Getting a grant to help him back to college was out of the question. He had to find something that paid better than hairdressing so he could save enough money to keep himself going while he studied. He heard that the Ford car plant at Halewood on the River Mersey paid good money to contract workers who were prepared to go up onto the roof girders high above the factory floor and clean off the oil that gathered and stuck there. There was no safety equipment and the work had to be done at night. Many people who went along took one look and left. But a few people, those as desperate as Willy Russell, stuck it out to earn good money. Some fell and were badly injured. He was lucky. When the college term started in September 1969, he had enough money to leave Ford and join the other students at Childwall.

The students around Willy Russell were all at least five years younger than he was. He says they thought he was a **CIA** spy, but as soon as they discovered that he played the guitar and wrote songs he was accepted. He even ran in the election to be president of the Student Union, and won. He left the college with six more O levels and an A level in English Literature. He knew that his year at Childwall was his last chance to gain qualifications and he did not let the chance slip by.

The Edinburgh Festival

Every August, Scotland's capital city hosts one of the greatest arts festivals in the world, attracting thousands of visitors each year. Theatre, music, film and comedy are especially well represented. Every space that can host a performance is crammed with shows and acts that follow one another from early morning to late at night. There are hundreds of events in theatres, halls, pubs and on the streets.

But more important than even the exams was the sense that finally he was moving towards his goal of being a writer. He had broken through the barriers that he felt surrounded working-class people. In 1969, he enrolled on a three-year full-time teacher-training course to be a drama teacher. It was his wife, Annie, who had advised him to study to be teacher. He was now in the position he had dreamed of while working in the hairdressing salon: that of a student with long holidays in which to write plays.

Blind Scouse

In 1971, he wrote the first short play that he thought was good enough to be produced on stage. *Keep Your Eyes Down* was performed as part of a student **production** at St Katherine's College where he was training. He then wrote another play called *Sam O'Shanker* that was also performed in the college.

These plays and another were gathered together under the title *Blind Scouse* and performed at the 1972 Edinburgh Arts Festival. It was a student production with no financial backing, but people were prepared to work for no money to produce plays at the world's greatest performing arts festival. Willy Russell was thoroughly involved in the production – he was not just the writer. He even acted in some of the student shows. (He has continued to do small amounts of acting throughout his life, and says he would do more 'if the right film part came along'.)

His practical ability to organize and get shows up and running had already been shown in the various folk clubs he had run in Liverpool. Student productions were fun and a chance for new writers to show their work, but everyone worked long hours for no money. But the show at the Edinburgh Festival was about to alter the course of his life.

23

The Liverpool Everyman

While Willy Russell was writing his first plays for student production, one of the professional theatres in Liverpool, the Liverpool Everyman, was putting on work that inspired and excited him. In particular, John McGrath's play *Unruly Elements*, staged at the Everyman, had reinforced his desire to write for the stage. Led by the **director** Alan Dosser and the **playwright** McGrath, the Everyman was trying to create a new type of theatre that would have direct appeal and relevance to the people of Liverpool. A lot of conventional theatre in the late 1960s was about **middle-class** life or aimed at middle-class audiences. Serious dramas set among the **working class** only appeared on television.

Willy Russell felt that in his plays written for the Liverpool Everyman, John McGrath 'really **exploited** the language of the common man to say major and universal things'. He saw McGrath doing in drama what the folk songs he played in the Liverpool clubs did in a different way – giving ordinary people voices to speak directly to others about their lives. But when Willy Russell sent an early play to the Liverpool Everyman, it was rejected.

The Liverpool Everyman Theatre, where Willy Russell found inspiration for his working-class dramas.

A little while later, Willy Russell was in Edinburgh with a student **company**. As luck would have it, John McGrath turned up at the Festival and went to see *Blind Scouse*. He loved it, and got Alan Dosser to come. The show was doing well and selling out, so the two men from the Everyman had to be squeezed into the tiny theatre where the play was performed.

The Liverpool Everyman today, still a working theatre making shows for the people of Liverpool.

Writing full-time

This was the start of a fruitful working partnership, as McGrath and Dosser wanted Willy Russell to write for their theatre. He was now teaching in a Liverpool comprehensive school, and writing in his spare time. They asked him to **adapt** a play by another playwright, Alan Plater, called *The Tigers are Coming OK*. It was the sort of play that interested Willy Russell, in which the misfortunes of a small, struggling football club are used throughout as an **extended metaphor** for the struggles of the leading character. Alan Dosser wanted Willy Russell to rewrite the play to make it more relevant to Liverpool audiences. The new version was called *When the Reds* (a reference to a Liverpool Football Club song) and opened at the Everyman in 1973. At the same time **commissions** for dramas for television began to come in and Willy Russell was able to give up teaching. Since 1974 he has made all his money from his imagination and his writing.

Success

Writing drama is not a very secure profession. You can write a hit show, but then find that no one is prepared to read, let alone invest in, your next one. But by 1974, Willy Russell realized he might actually be able to make a career out of his writing. The energy, drive and self-belief he had shown in fighting to get himself an education were still strong in him. A brave move would lead him to his first stage hit.

A successful musical

John, Paul, George, Ringo… and Bert is, of course, about the Beatles, and about a man (Bert) who has had a life-long obsession with them. The Contact Theatre in Manchester (a city often regarded as Liverpool's rival as well as neighbour) wanted to do a documentary drama about the Beatles. They had a script but it had no original dialogue, just pieces of interviews with the Beatles inserted between their songs that made up most of the show. Alan Dosser wanted Willy Russell to do something with the piece and then bring it to the Everyman in the Beatles' home city. Willy Russell said he believed he could write a much better piece about the group. Dosser gave him the chance to prove it.

John, Paul, George, Ringo… and Bert starts with a bold piece of theatre. A group **busk** Beatles' songs out in the street as the audience enter the theatre. The group follow the audience into the building, through the **auditorium**, and go up onto the stage. They are the band in the show. Bert then gives a review of the Beatles' lives and rise to fame. The show contained two original songs, written by Willy Russell.

The company of *John, Paul, George, Ringo… and Bert*. Can you identify the Beatles look-alikes?

The West End

The West End of London has more theatres for its size than anywhere else in the world (Broadway in New York is a close second), and **playwrights** consider it a major achievement to get their work into one of them. A lot of musicals are staged in the West End – visitors like to 'take in a show' when they are in London, and a big musical with dances, great songs and spectacular effects is the sort of evening out many of them enjoy. Some musicals can run for years and years, playing to a full house every night.

Most plays and musicals do not start off in the West End. They are staged in a regional theatre like the Everyman in Liverpool. Then, after they have had any problems sorted out and rewrites done, they are moved to London. It is very expensive to put on a West End show, especially a musical, and if the audiences don't come, or if the **critics** don't like it, a lot of money can be lost very quickly.

London's 'theatre-land', the West End of London. Every night, over 30 theatres put on plays and musicals.

It was a risk, but one that paid off hugely for everyone involved in the show, because the piece that Willy Russell wrote soon became a hit. *John, Paul, George, Ringo… and Bert* quickly transferred to the West End of London and won two awards for Best New Musical. It ran in London for over a year, playing to full houses night after night.

Television and radio

At the same time that *John, Paul, George, Ringo... and Bert* was becoming a hit on stage, Willy Russell's dramas began to be broadcast on television. In fact, the early television scripts had been read and accepted by the BBC before he had his stage hit. His name was becoming well-known. It was literally 'up in lights' on a theatre in London. His **agent**, Peggy Ramsey, helped him plan his writing career. She was famous in the theatre world for the way she drove and encouraged the writers she represented.

Through the medium of television, Willy Russell's plays reached a much larger audience. In the mid-1970s, television companies, especially the BBC, which has made most of Willy Russell's television dramas, were eager to find new talented writers, particularly from outside London. Willy Russell's first television piece, *King of the Castle*, was broadcast in 1973 as part of a series called *Second City Firsts*

A scene from Willy Russell's television play *King of the Castle*.

Radio drama

As well as producing plays for the television, the BBC is also the world's major producer of radio drama. It broadcasts a play every day of the year. Willy Russell wrote a drama for radio – *I Read the News Today* (named after a Beatles song) – which was broadcast on BBC Schools Radio in 1977. As with some of his television work, radio producers saw that his plays about young people worked not just as adult entertainment, but had direct appeal to young people themselves. They saw that Willy Russell did something that many writers could not quite get right – he portrayed young people that young people themselves could believe in and identify with.

Other television and BBC radio **commissions** quickly followed: *Break-In*, a BBC *Play for Schools* in 1974, and *Death of a Young Young Man*, for the prestigious BBC *Play for Today* slot, in the same year.

(new or first-time plays from cities other than the capital). Because his plays were so firmly rooted in Liverpool and the way **Liverpudlians** behaved and talked, Willy Russell's work exactly fitted the bill for this series.

Being a writer is a risky business. There is no 'job security'. It is often said that writers are only ever as good as their last book. Writing drama is even more risky, as putting a show on stage involves so many things besides the script (for example, good acting, **directing**, design) that have to be right for the whole **production** to be a success. *John, Paul, George, Ringo… and Bert* was a huge success. It was popular, drawing big audiences, and was well reviewed by the theatre critics in the newspapers. It was a great achievement for a writer who was really just starting out on his career.

While he was enjoying his professional success, private life brought its own pleasures. His first child, Robert, was born in 1974 (followed by Ruth in 1977 and Rachel in 1980).

One for the Road

The popular image of Liverpool is of a city full of comedians, of a people who laugh their way through difficult times. Willy Russell's work has certainly contributed to this image. Most of his scripts contain a lot of humour. But *One for the Road*, which opened on stage in Manchester in 1976, is perhaps his most out-and-out comic play. It has endless running jokes, comic surprises and physical humour. He recalls writing the play almost as a test of how long comedy can be constantly kept going with just four characters sitting in a room.

One for the Road pokes fun at the way **working-class** people behave when they 'get on'. It is set on a new housing estate, not a poor, inner-city estate troubled by crime and vandalism, but a smart development of 'executive **dormer** bungalows', where the owners desperately try to be **middle class**. It takes place over the course of one evening when two couples have a dinner party. All but one of them appears happy with their new life, with gardening and the residents' association. Dennis, however, wants to be a rebel, but his rebellion consists of finally admitting to being the terror of 'phase two' of the housing development. He goes round at night knocking the heads off ornamental garden gnomes and spray-painting peoples' vegetables in vivid colours.

Unlike the women who rebel in Willy Russell's plays (Linda, Rita and Shirley Valentine), Dennis does not ultimately get away to a different, freer life, as he boasts he will. He settles for routine and quiet – the certain future of his marriage and the estate. *One for the Road* tells a comic story that is almost a traditional **farce**, but it has a serious, sad message – that people become trapped in lives they don't really want. The residents of the estate may have escaped from the difficulties of inner-city life, their new 'success' may be more comfortable, but it is equally hollow. Beyond the comedy, it is a bleak story.

The young old

Russell calls the characters that live on the estate the *young old*. They are roughly the same age as he was when he wrote the play, but have settled down to a life of quiet desperation. Willy Russell was not living

Roger begins this speech by trying to persuade his friend Dennis that running away from life on the estate is a bad idea. By the end he's changed his mind – but neither of them ever leave!

'Come off it. You're not goin' anywhere an' you know it… Don't be soft. Even if you were serious and you did go, have you thought what it would be like? Eh? What would you be doin' eh? While we'd be here sleepin' under warm continental quilts, you'd be out there kipping in the grass or the sand. While we'd be at good tables, eating good food you'd be sittin' round some bloody camp fire. While we'd be comin' home every night to the same wife an' the same house there wouldn't be the same security for you. You wouldn't have responsibilities. Life would just be an endless list of different places and new encounters an' fresh women. Christ, you lucky bugger. I'll get us a beer.'

on a new estate like his characters. The success of his writing had allowed him and his young family to buy a **Victorian** terraced house in Liverpool. Although he was becoming well-known, even famous, he still lived an 'ordinary life', the sort of day-to-day existence he might have been living had he stayed a teacher. He did the shopping, helped with the children, but went to his study each day to write plays.

Modern houses on the sort of suburban estate where Willy Russell set *One for the Road*. The play is based on the idea that such places create a certain mind set, a need to conform, in the minds of the people that move there.

A writer's life

By the late 1970s, Willy Russell was one of the most popular **playwrights** in Britain. A new stage play, *Breezeblock Park*, had opened at the Liverpool Everyman in 1975 and then transferred to London. His first play for commercial television, *The Daughters of Albion*, was broadcast in 1978. So what sort of life does a successful playwright lead?

They work a lot! They sit at their desk, inventing characters and stories. Willy Russell can write quickly, without planning or note-making, letting the characters come alive and propel the plot forward. But like any writer he can also suffer 'writer's block', when the ideas and words just won't come. He has followed the advice of his first **agent**, Peggy Ramsey, who encouraged so many great writers at the start of their careers. She said that hard work was the only way and that the creative writing process 'might not happen when you are at your desk, but it certainly won't happen if you're not'.

Because he is interested not just in writing the script for a play, but in the whole process of casting, rehearsal and **production**, Willy Russell

Willy Russell, by now a successful playwright, photographed for a theatre programme for one of his shows in the mid-1970s.

has always spent a lot of time in theatres while his shows are being prepared for performance. He is keen to take part in the casting process to decide which actors will play his characters. He rewrites scenes during rehearsals, and even cuts or changes lines after the show has opened to the public. When he has a show running in a theatre he will see it every week or so to begin with, just to make sure there is no more rewriting he can do to make it work even better.

In the 1970s, Willy Russell and his family lived in the Newsham Park area of Liverpool. This was a pleasant, ordinary area such as you might find close to the centre of any British city, made up of streets of terraced and semi-detached Victorian and Edwardian houses, mainly owned by young professional families.

Family man

When he was not working at his desk, in theatre rehearsals or in television studios, Willy Russell did the same things that any family man would do. He took the children to school, did the shopping, stayed in and watched television. He thinks that sometimes people saw him in the supermarket and thought that he, the 'great playwright', must just be doing this to remind himself how the ordinary people, who form the basis for most of his famous characters, live. In fact, he was just getting the food!

People might like to think that a writer as successful as Willy Russell would go out and buy all sorts of expensive things. In fact, he is not **materialistic** and says that as soon as he started earning money from his writing he easily acquired everything he wanted: a good stereo to listen to music, a guitar to play and compose music on, and a Volvo, because as a responsible father of three young children, he wanted to have the safest car on the road!

Our Day Out

Our Day Out was **commissioned** by the BBC and first shown on television the day after Boxing Day in 1976. It is a very funny account of a school outing from Liverpool to North Wales by the 'progress class', the pupils who are having difficulty mastering basic skills. The drama of the piece, however, conveys a serious and sad message about how these young people are regarded, even by some of their teachers.

Christmas is a time when television companies try to outdo each other for the biggest share of viewers. People often watch more television around Christmas than at any other time of the year. Companies put on the best programmes they can. It was a great achievement to have a play broadcast at this time that, though comic, has a tough message about how 'the system' can damage the chances of poor or not so bright young people. The newspaper reviewers loved its mix of comedy and seriousness – *The Daily Express*, for example, called it 'A trip that shouldn't be missed'.

Within six weeks it was re-broadcast in the BBC's **flagship** *Play for Today* slot. It was shown again in 1979. Then, in 1983, it was **adapted** for stage and put on at the Liverpool Everyman Theatre.

Just shoot

The cast needs ten young people between the ages of twelve and fifteen to take speaking parts, plus a lot more to make up class numbers on the school trip. Many

A scene from the television version of *Our Day Out*, Willy Russell's hugely successful drama about Liverpool school kids on a day trip to Wales.

Real life humour

Much of the popularity of *Our Day Out* was due to the comedy, which was both in the lines spoken and in the actions that happen in the film. A screenwriter has to be able to imagine and describe the events he wants to happen as well as give the actors words to speak. Here is an extract from a scene from *Our Day Out*, where the school group have 'borrowed' a lot of small animals from a zoo. They are setting off on the coach when:

KEEPER: *(Pushing onto the coach)* Right.
Come on. Where are they? *(The KIDS look back innocently.)*
Call yourselves teachers. You can't even control them.

TEACHER: Now look. This has gone far enough.
Would you tell me exactly what you want please?

(A clucking hen is heard. The KEEPER turns and looks. A KID is fidgeting with his coat. The KEEPER strides up to him and pulls back his coat, revealing a bantam hen. Two more KEEPERS come on board. The first KEEPER grabs the hen and addresses the KIDS.)

KEEPER: Right! And now I want the rest!

*(There is a moment's hesitation before the flood-gates are opened. Animals appear from every conceivable hiding place. The coach becomes a **menagerie**. Mrs KAY raises her eyebrows to heaven. The KEEPER collects the animals.)*

writers and directors are wary of working with young people ('Never work with children or animals' is an old theatrical warning!) but Willy Russell loved working with the kids. Although he drew on his experience of teaching, the play was one that just flowed onto the page – it was written in only four days. The characters are so powerful that they drive the story along. The director who was shooting the film complained that there was nothing to do except shoot. He meant there was no need to have discussions with the writer about how to improve scenes, or to think about how things could be changed.

Stags and Hens

In 1978, Willy Russell's powerful and unusual play *Stags and Hens* opened at the Everyman Theatre in Liverpool. It is set in the lavatories of a run-down nightclub on the eve of the marriage of Dave and Linda, two **working-class Liverpudlians**. Superstition says that the bride and groom are not supposed to see one another on the night before their wedding, but Dave's stag night and Linda's hen night have been accidentally planned for this same club.

By the end of the evening, the boys have given their 'view' of marriage and how married women should behave, and the girls have told Linda how wonderful life will be, though to her it sounds more like a prison. Linda breaks out of the gent's toilet window and runs away with the singer of the group that were booked to be playing at the club that night. Dave, her now jilted groom, spends the whole play unconscious through drink, with his head in the toilet!

Although there is lots of humour in the writing, the play is a powerful attack on the way young working-class people regard marriage. Linda sees that her youth will be taken away when she gets married. She says to her friend 'It's not just like I'm marryin' Dave. It's like if I marry him I marry everythin'. Like, I could sit down now and draw you a

---

Writing a play

Stags and Hens was written very quickly. Willy Russell had had the idea for the story for ages, but once he began writing the characters the writing just took off. Although he is a **meticulous** craftsman, constantly rewriting and often cutting lines from his plays, he tries to let 'inspiration' drive him quickly through the first draft of a new play. At this stage in the writing, he doesn't believe in stopping to do research, nor in planning out scenes in advance. He says of both *Educating Rita* and *Shirley Valentine* that when he began writing them he had no real idea 'what sort of character would walk onto the page as I wrote the play'.

chart of everthin' that'll happen in my life after tomorrow.' Rita in *Educating Rita* will echo this when she says that educated people 'stay younger longer'.

Stags and Hens was a very important play for Russell. It became a huge hit on stage and has been **adapted** as a screenplay, called *Dancing Thru' the Dark*. It had to be completely rewritten to open out the action from the two lavatories that form the **set** on stage.

The working class

Willy Russell wrote *Stags and Hens* when he was Fellow in Creative Writing at Manchester Polytechnic (1977–79). This sort of post is given to writers seen to have skill and talent, and is a sign of public recognition. The writer encourages students interested in creative writing to develop their own skills and talents. It is also supposed to give writers who are struggling to make a living the time to write. When *Stags and Hens* was completed, it was performed by Polytechnic students on a closed circuit television network in the college: an ingenious idea that combined Willy Russell's interest in stage and television.

Harsh reality

In many ways *Stags and Hens* is the least comic, harshest play Willy Russell has written. The boys are narrow-minded, poorly educated and capable of being vicious and violent. They try to dominate the girls, and treat them with contempt. The girls allow themselves to be **demeaned** in this way and seem (apart from Linda) hopelessly locked into a narrow, repressed future as wives of poorly behaved men.

Willy Russell did not set out simply to attack young working-class people, but he wanted to present a true picture of the sort of lives many felt themselves resigned to lead. He has never romanticized the working-class characters he has created in his plays. However, *Stags and Hens* was condemned by many people as painting an unsympathetic portrait of a whole class of people. The **Socialist** Worker's Party condemned the play. Willy Russell in turn condemns his critics for being **middle-class** people with no real experience of working-class life. They were 'taking the side of the working class' at a time when in many ways traditional class divisions and life styles were disappearing, especially in cities like Liverpool.

"
In this extract, Robbie recalls being shocked by a girl asking for a beer and not a 'girl's drink' in the pub. Notice how he insultingly refers to the girls as 'tarts' and how he thinks Dave should 'control' the girl he is taking out.
"

ROBBIE: I was goin' out with this cracking tart once, y'know, nice, smart girl she was. We went out on a foursome with Dave and his tart. I got the first round in, asking them what they were havin'. This girl I'm with she said er, a Babycham or a Pony or somethin', y'know, a proper tart's drink. Know what Dave's tart asked for eh? A pint of bitter. That's dead true that, she wasn't jokin'. I was dead embarrassed. I'm out with this nice girl for the first time and Dave's tart's actin' like a docker. I said to Dave after, fancy letting your tart behave like that.
From Willy Russell's *Stags and Hens*

Willy Russell knows enough about the realities of working-class life to understand that many people stifle their own chances of success by accepting what other people tell them is going to be their lot in life. He has no time for this. He also understands that to use the term 'working class' to define a huge number and range of people who happen to work in certain jobs to earn their living is foolish. There were a number of great working-class 'heroes' written by different authors in various books, plays and films in the 1950s and 1960s, but Willy Russell rightly observes that if these fictional characters could all meet together, they would be so different that they would have very little to say to one another. It is people from outside the so-called working class, the people who criticized the realities he wrote about in *Stags and Hens*, who often seem to see working-class people as one big group.

In the late 1970s, when Willy Russell was writing *Stags and Hens*, there were many strikes, some of them, like this, in Liverpool. Middle-class political **radicals** and others supported this 'working-class struggle', but their view of who the working class actually were was not as clear as Willy Russell's. When they saw his realistic portrayal of young working-class people in *Stags and Hens* many of them were angry.

In his own words

Willy Russell gave up singing and playing his guitar in small folk clubs in the mid-1970s, although he still wrote new songs. By this time, he was able to buy better homes for his family and employ **agents** and assistants to deal with all the business that resulted from the success of his writing, such as details of **productions** of his plays and the publication of scripts. He also began travelling a lot to work at rehearsals in Britain and Europe. One of his few luxuries is that he always travels first-class and stays in good hotels!

Although he has many friends in the 'business', including world-famous theatre actors, he has many 'ordinary' friends and spends a lot of evenings at home in front of the TV with a bottle of wine. He has never become a remote and aloof 'great writer'. In interviews and in the notes he writes for programmes for productions of his plays he demonstrates the down-to-earth humour that comes out in so many of his fictional characters.

Here is Willy Russell talking about life and writing, 'in his own words'.

> "
> 'Perhaps my introduction should be an attempt to win your sympathy… by outlining the agony I endured, the sleepless nights I spent, the terror I knew and the emptiness I sometimes felt when struggling to write these plays. But why inflict that on you? No doubt you too have your own struggles, your own terror and here you are, you've just got through the door having been sacked from your job, your spouse has recently left you, the dog's got worms, the Tories are still in power, the telly's bust, the radio's full of programmes about the nuclear winter (apart from the local commercial station, which just sounds like a nuclear winter) and you open this slim volume, just to read a few plays, and what do you get? Some pillock called the author whingein' on about the agony of writing a play…'
> "
> Willy Russell, from the introduction to a collection of his works, 1986

'In the morning, (I'm) bog-eyed and trembling, staggering down to the kitchen to find the kids already up, attacking the Coco Pops and each other. Filling the kettle... trying to apply futile liberal ideas to the kids' uncomplicated brutality. 'That's mine', 'No it's not', 'Well I'm not gonna be your friend, ever!' A normal sort of morning, something like a session at the United Nations, with breakfast cereal.'

Willy Russell, from the introduction to a collection of his works, 1986

Willy Russell in 1987, a successful writer, looking very pleased with the way things are going!

Educating Rita

The now world-famous play (and film) *Educating Rita* was first staged in 1980, and it has become one of Willy Russell's best-known works. It contains more autobiographical material than anything else he has written. Rita (who later in the play returns to her real name, Susan) is a hairdresser. She has the same job that Willy Russell had as a young man, and she speaks with the authentic voice of a **working-class Liverpudlian** woman – the sort of voice he would have heard everyday in the hairdressing salon. And Rita, in her twenties, struggles to get the education she missed at school – just as Willy Russell did.

Educating Rita was **commissioned** by the Royal Shakespeare Company, one of the greatest theatre companies in the world, and premiered at The Warehouse, their London studio venue (a small theatre attached to a bigger one). By this stage, Willy Russell did not open his plays in Liverpool or any other provincial city, hoping they would then transfer to the capital – he opened right in the heart of London itself. *Educating Rita* quickly transferred to the Piccadilly Theatre, a bigger theatre in the West End, and played to crowded houses for three years. It was a huge critical and commercial success.

A powerful story

To people who have only seen the film version (which came out in 1983) it may come as a shock to learn that the stage version has only two actors (Rita/Susan and Frank, her university tutor) and that it all takes place in his office at the university. In that sense, *Educating Rita* is a small, intimate play, but it tells a story of big ideas, ideas close to Willy Russell's heart. Although there is, as always, a lot of humour in the writing, it is a deadly serious play, about class and choice. It is also very easy to understand, a factor which was a prime concern for the author. 'I wanted to make a play which engaged and was relevant to those who considered themselves uneducated, those whose daily language is not the language of the university or the theatre. I wanted to write a play which would attract, and be as valid for, the Ritas in the audience as the Franks.'

> *I love stories. I spend all my writing life trying to make stories... A story, like a song, can transcend barriers of language, class and race... I hope you will find Educating Rita understandable without lengthy analysis... and I hope you will not think me lowbrow [unthinking], unsound or inferior when I tell you that when making Educating Rita I tried very hard to write a love story. I hope I did.*
> Willy Russell, on stories

As we have seen, Willy Russell's *John, Paul, George, Ringo... and Bert* had been a big hit in the early 1970s, and several of his plays for television had been very well reviewed. But it was the huge success of *Educating Rita*, a play with such a simple, powerful story, that really made Willy Russell's name as a successful and popular **playwright**.

Educating Rita was such a successful stage play that, during its long run, five different actresses played Rita. Julie Walters (above) also played Rita in the film version.

Rita on the big screen

Many stage plays are as successful as *Educating Rita* was during its West End run, but few are so suitable for **adaptation** into film. Its heroine is exactly the sort of person who, in real life, would not go to the theatre (either out of choice or because a theatre ticket is usually quite expensive) but might go to the cinema. And it is a very funny play, which broadens its appeal to a cinema audience.

Some authors (especially if they write novels) let a professional screen writer adapt their work into a film script, but Willy Russell wrote his own new version of *Educating Rita* for filming. Film can tell a story in very different ways to a stage play. In Willy Russell's adaptation, we see all the characters that Frank and Rita only talk about on stage. Many new scenes are added, taking advantage of the fact that a film can move from **location** to location. So we see the hairdressing salon, and the contrasting homes of Rita and Frank. Ironically for a writer who sets all his plays in Liverpool, all the university and outdoor scenes were actually shot in Dublin!

Willy Russell was keen to ensure that the intimacy of the play's original structure was not lost in a film that was set in many different locations. The simple one-room **set** of the play had framed the events that took place in the story, and a key part of Rita's visits were her reports of what was happening in the rest of her life that we didn't see. So in the film, the images of the university campus, and the changing seasons we see from the window of Frank's study, create a new 'frame' for the story of Frank and Rita's lives.

International success

The film version of *Educating Rita* starred Michael Caine and Julie Walters, and it was a huge hit. Willy Russell's screenplay was nominated for an Academy Award (an 'Oscar') and most reviewers praised the film for its warmth, humour and honesty. But international fame is not without its frustrations. A few reviewers in America showed just how little they knew about the plot of the play and English life. One complained that the film was shot in Dublin when of course it

Julie Walters as the part-time student Rita and Michael Caine as Frank, her university tutor, in a scene from the film version of *Educating Rita*. She is looking pleased with an essay she has just handed in, he is less sure! (See exerpt from the script below.)

should be London – despite the fact that Rita has a strong Liverpool accent and is obviously living in the town where she grew up! Another said that Frank finally 'does himself in' – suggesting that he kills himself – which is why the love between Rita and Frank does not develop, when in fact Frank is sent on 'study leave' to Australia.

> " FRANK: I want to talk about this that you sent me. (He holds a sheet of A4 paper.) "
>
> RITA: That? Oh.
>
> FRANK: Yes. In response to the question 'Suggest how you would resolve the staging difficulties inherent in a production of Ibsen's Peer Gynt', you have written 'Do it on the radio...'
>
> From Willy Russell's *Educating Rita*

Blood Brothers

Willy Russell had the very general idea for *Blood Brothers*, the most successful musical he has ever composed, in his head for years. Since its first performance in 1983, it has won more awards than any other musical in the history of British theatre. But the way Willy Russell remembers it, the show finally came about through two 'magic' moments. The first one was due to his six-year-old daughter Ruthie.

For several years he had dreamed of a musical where he wrote the script (called the 'book' in a musical), the music and the lyrics for the songs: in fact the whole thing! (Usually musicals are written collaboratively, with different people doing these parts.) Although he had had a major hit on the London West End stage with his musical *John, Paul, George, Ringo... and Bert*, trying to do the whole thing himself was going to be a huge challenge.

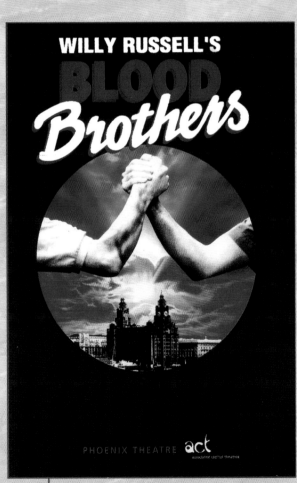

In his early life, before becoming a professional **playwright**, Willy Russell had written hundreds of songs and performed them in clubs in Liverpool. But none of these songs were, by his own admission, really remembered by anybody.

A poster for the UK production of *Blood Brothers*.

Are you hummable?

One day Willy Russell was talking to his **agent** about his desire to write everything for a musical. She looked at him and said: 'In musical theatre you must, absolutely must, be hummable.' She was pointing out the fact that to be successful, a musical must have at least one or two songs that the audience can come out of the performance humming.

One day he had sent his children to school, and was sitting down, drinking a cup of coffee. Suddenly he realized that he had hardly noticed, in all the chaos of a busy morning, that his daughter Ruthie had been humming – humming one of his tunes! He says that he rushed down to the school playground in his slippers and made her hum the tune again just to make sure it was actually one of his.

Some of the most famous songs in popular music history have been written for musicals. The lyrics are very important because they must not only work within the song, but also connect to the overall story that is being told on stage. Lyricists like Ira Gershwin wrote brilliant and cunningly rhymed lyrics. Gershwin wrote the lyrics for a song called 'It Ain't Necessarily So' in which he talks about Jonah, the biblical character supposedly swallowed by a whale. Gershwin says:

'That man made his home in
a fish's abdomen.' (You have to say it as ab-*dome*-in!)

> "
> *'Quickly, I say (to my daughter), hum me a few bars of that tune.
> And suddenly I'm jumping up and down in the school playground
> shrieking with delight because one of my kids has picked up a melody
> of mine. I'm shouting "Hummable, hummable" over and over again.
> Other kids are looking at me as though I'm a fully fledged nut and
> teachers are streaming from all directions to apprehend a man gone
> mad... After satisfying the Headmaster that I am a mere parent
> suffering with nothing more dangerous than Chronic-Desire-to-Write-a-
> Musical he instructs the caretaker and the* **peripatetic** *music teacher
> to release their grip on me...'*
> "
> Willy Russell, from the introduction to a collection of his works, 1986

The story

Willy Russell knew he could write songs that would make a successful musical. But what would the story be about? The best musicals have very simple plots. *Blood Brothers* is about twins secretly parted at birth. They only learn the truth about their identity the day they are killed as the result of an argument between themselves. It is a very simple story, almost like an ancient myth. As Willy Russell says: 'It feels as if it's a story that's always existed... But in fact I was walking along one day and didn't have an idea of the story, then I took the next step and I had it. It just came out of the blue. The whole story was there.' This was the second 'magic moment'. He clearly believes in inspiration!

Now came the hard work. He had to bring this basic plot to life, to create characters that people would care about and believe in as they watched the show. For a world-famous musical, *Blood Brothers* had humble beginnings. Willy Russell wrote the work, which lasted just over an hour and had just one song, for the Merseyside Young People's Theatre Company. It toured round schools and was watched by young people.

A scene from the 1995 London production of *Blood Brothers* at the Phoenix Theatre. Edward (Carl Wayne) is talking to Mrs Johnstone (Barbara Dickson). Edward is the son Mrs Johnstone was forced to give away as a baby, who has now become great friends with the son she kept and brought up. Edward likes his best friend's mother, and does not know that she is kind to him because she is his real mother.

A photograph to celebrate the tenth anniversary of *Blood Brothers*. The stars pictured include (left to right): Andy Snowden, Keith Burns, Lyn Paul, Willy Russell, Kiki Dee, Bill Kenwright (the producer), Debbie Paul and Mark Hutchinson.

Agony and torture

It was a year before a new full-length version was written and ready to go into Liverpool Playhouse Theatre. Willy Russell has described the process of writing a play as sometimes being 'agony' and 'like torture'. He admits to having sleepless nights when things don't go right. With this new full-length version of *Blood Brothers*, he knew a lot of money would be invested, and if the show flopped it would be a disaster. He had to get it right. With his other great successes, the plays *Educating Rita* and *Shirley Valentine*, he remembers starting with the main character and letting the story develop as he went along. With *Blood Brothers* he had the whole story worked out, and needed to invent characters to bring it to life.

Willy Russell is a skilled and experienced theatre writer, and likes to submit a script that is ready for the director and actors to work on. In the case of *Blood Brothers*, this meant having all the music ready for the band to play in rehearsals.

He then watches how the show develops in rehearsals and does re-writes to get it ready for performance. After *Blood Brothers* had been running for three months in Liverpool he persuaded the director to let him cut fifteen minutes from the end of Act Two to tighten up the story.

The now slightly shorter musical moved on to London where it became a huge hit, and since then it has been produced by different theatres worldwide. Musicals as successful as this develop a sort of life of their own, apart from the author. Willy Russell has said he has stopped even thinking of doing any more rewrites.

Writing songs

Willy Russell's song-writing goes back to his youth in the 1960s when he wrote and performed songs in small folk clubs around Liverpool. He jokes about writing such long-forgotten classics as 'The Mersey Tunnel is three miles long and the roof is made of glass'! But for *Blood Brothers* he knew he had to compose the best music and lyrics he possibly could.

The original version of *Blood Brothers* had been shown to possibly the most demanding audience of all – school children. During its tour through schools in and around Liverpool it was seen by 8000 'young critics'. Willy Russell wrote about them in the programme for the full stage version of the play: 'Many of them had written to myself and the company to say how much the piece had meant to them. I knew that if I got the (new version of) the musical wrong they wouldn't hesitate to write again to tell me it was "crap", "last" or "lousy".'

The original version they saw ran for 70 minutes, had just one song, and had taken five weeks to write. For the big stage version Willy Russell needed around a dozen songs. This was like starting the musical all over again.

> "
> *'I was expecting to work at my usual (comparatively) fast rate but wasn't prepared for the unique demands of the musical form… I'd rattle through the dialogue doing up to ten pages a day, then I'd get to a point that demanded a song and I'd spend up to two weeks on it. It was fascinating and seductive. Sometimes I deliberately found excuses not to finish a song so that I could prolong the process of working in miniature.'*
> "
> Willy Russell, on writing songs

'Writing a song is like solving a crossword puzzle with melody and lyrics. You compose the right melody and then:

   a) You know what you have to say in the song.

   b) You have to carry the plot forward.

   c) You want it to be perfectly phrased and rhymed.

Of course what often happens is that you can say what you want but can't get it to rhyme. Or you get a cheap rhyme which doesn't say what you want – it's a thoroughly exhausting but ultimately satisfying process.'

Willy Russell, on writing songs

'Tell Me It's Not True'

Songs may look simple when written down, but can take days and days to get right. Rhymes are important. Look at the rhymes in this song (below), which is sung at the tragic climax of *Blood Brothers*.

Tell me it's not true
Say it's just a story
Something on the news
Tell me it's not true
Though it's here before me
Say it's just a dream
Say it's just a scene
From an old movie of
   years ago
From an old movie of
   Marilyn Monroe
Say it's just some clowns
Two players in the limelight
And bring the curtain down
Say it's just two clowns
Who couldn't get their
   lines right
Say it's just a show

On the radio
That we can turn over
   and start again
That we can turn over,
   it's only a game

Tell me it's not true
Say I only dreamed it
And morning will come soon
Tell me it's not true
Say you didn't mean it
Say it's just pretend
Say it's just the end
Of an old movie from
   years ago
Of an old movie with
   Marilyn Monroe

Shirley Valentine

Being the author of a world-class successful musical brings pressures and responsibilities. Willy Russell attended castings for new **productions** as well as rehearsals and opening nights of the show in many different countries. But as a writer he needed to develop new creative ideas. In 1986, he completed a play called *Shirley Valentine*. It was very different from *Blood Brothers*. It was a one-woman show, with no songs. It was in some ways a small show, but dealt with big ideas.

Shirley Valentine is a middle-aged woman who goes on a two-week package holiday without telling her husband and doesn't come home. The play has some themes in common with *Educating Rita*. Both plays feature women struggling to experience more of life than their husbands want them to – and both women break free. But the 40-something-year-old Shirley is a very different character from the 26-year-old Rita. Shirley sees that her husband, a middle-aged man running a small business, is just as trapped in his daily life as she is in hers, but he hasn't seen it. One of her key lines comes when she recognizes that she is at least partly responsible for the life she is unhappily leading, and she says 'At least it would be easier if I had someone to blame.'

One-woman show

In *Shirley Valentine*, Willy Russell again moved into a new style of writing – the one-woman show. Although when it was made into a film it had a full cast and was shot on **location** in Liverpool and Greece, the original stage play was written for one voice. In the first act, when she is at home in Liverpool, Shirley is always alone in her kitchen, talking to the wall. In the second act she is alone on a Greek beach, talking to a rock. Shirley is a lonely and unfulfilled woman. The play has tremendous power because the actor always speaks directly to the audience, as if we are eavesdropping on her conversations to the wall or the rock.

Stage vs cinema

The play opened in Liverpool in March 1986 and did not appear in London until January 1988. It starred Pauline Collins, who went on to play Shirley in the film version, which was shot in 1989. The film's director was Lewis Gilbert, who directed the film of *Educating Rita*. Turning the play into a film involved a complete rewrite. Like the film version of *Educating Rita*, the film version of *Shirley Valentine* is almost a different work to the stage original. It has two very powerful male characters (Shirley's husband and Costas, the Greek taverna owner) who are only talked about in the stage version.

Willy Russell enjoys being part of the filming process, but says that there is less to do for a writer on a film **set**. He is keenly involved in casting, the choosing of actors to play the parts, but the sheer cost of filming means that there is less time for experimentation and creative rehearsals than in the theatre, where the writer can be much more involved in making the show.

Pauline Collins as Shirley, the woman who 'finds herself' while on holiday on a Greek island, and Tom Conti as Costas the Greek, the man who befriends her, in the 1989 film version of *Shirley Valentine*.

The famous author today

Willy Russell works in two spacious offices on the top floors of a big house that has been converted into work spaces near Liverpool city centre. From the window you can see Liverpool Cathedral and the city streets that lead down to the famous River Mersey, the Pierhead and the Mersey ferry.

On one floor is a grand piano; on the other, desks with computers for writing. He tries to work from ten to five every day. At night he goes home to a cottage on the outskirts of the city, where, if he is working on something new or is 'inspired', he can carry on writing, playing or composing in another office.

He has so many books in print and **productions** of shows running that he has **agents** and assistants to deal with 'the business'. He has just published his first novel. Like many of his plays, *The Wrong Boy* is both funny and tragic. It shows how life, its accidents and unfortunate coincidences, can harm young people, forcing them into a way of life they haven't chosen and don't want.

Going back to song-writing and lyrics, the form his first creative writing took, he is now writing and recording an album of songs.

An honest voice

Willy Russell sometimes teaches Arvon residential writing courses. These are week-long residential courses where new writers are encouraged by successful professional authors to develop their talents. He believes very strongly that, in the business of play-writing, new or young writers need all the help they can get. He is sent many scripts by hopeful writers and tries to read and comment on these.

But writing is always a struggle. For Willy Russell, being a writer is being in a perpetual state of 'writer's block', in which you are always wrestling to bring ideas to life. He says that as a writer 'You can have ambition, but realize that your work is not achieving that ambition. Then it's agony.'

But whether achieved through agony, inspiration or long hours at his desk, Willy Russell creates through his characters a voice for 'ordinary people' that is honest, insightful and never patronizing. Just like this story that Rita tells her tutor in *Educating Rita*:

'I went into a pub an' they (her family) were singin', all of them singin' some song they'd learnt from the juke box. And I stood in that pub an' thought just what the frig am I trying to do? Why don't I just pack it [the university course] in an' stay with them, an' join in the singin... ? Well I did join in. But when I looked round, me mother had stopped singin' an' she was cryin'... Everyone just said she was pissed an' we should get her home. So we did, an' on the way I asked her why. I said "Why are y' cryin' mother?" She said "Because – because we could sing better songs than those."'

Willy Russell sharing the stage at the Liverpool Everyman Theatre with another famous Liverpudlian, former Beatle Paul McCartney. They were performing together at a poetry reading in 2001.

Timeline

This timeline contains key dates in Willy Russell's life and career, and important dates connected with Willy Russell's home city of Liverpool.

1947 Born in Whiston, between Liverpool and St Helens.

1952 Moves with family to Knowsley, on the outskirts of Liverpool.

1960 The Beatles form in Liverpool.

1962 Leaves school with one O level.
Fails printer's apprenticeship exam.
Enrols in college to become a ladies' hairdresser.
Writes songs in his spare time.

1963 'Beatlemania' is at its height. The group and Liverpool are world famous. The 'Mersey beat' (a term describing the music of The Beatles and other Liverpool groups) is the most popular form of pop music in the UK, if not the world.

1963–8 Trains then works as a ladies' hairdresser in Liverpool. Continues writing songs and stories.

1966 Meets Annie Seagroatt, who later becomes his wife.

1967 A best-selling anthology of ground-breaking poetry by three young Liverpool poets (Roger McGough, Adrian Henri and Brian Patten) is published.

1968 Gains entry to Childwall College and studies for O and A levels.

1969 The Beatles split up.

1970 Begins training to become a drama teacher.
Begins writing one-act plays.
Marries Annie.

1972 Three short plays, collectively titled *Blind Scouse*, are premiered at the Edinburgh Festival. They are seen and liked by established **playwright** John McGrath and theatre director Alan Dosser.

1973 Asked by the Everyman Theatre in Liverpool to adapt a stage play by writer Alan Plater (to make it more relevant to the Liverpool audience). He writes the play, which is called *When the Reds*.

1973 His first play for television, *King of the Castle*, is broadcast.

1974 *John, Paul, George, Ringo... and Bert*, a musical, becomes his first big hit. It transfers to London's West End.
Death of a Young Young Man is broadcast on television.
Son Robert is born.

1975 *Breezeblock Park* opens at the Everyman Theatre in Liverpool, then transfers to London.
Break In is produced by BBC Schools Television.

1976 *One for the Road* opens in Manchester.
Our Day Out is broadcast on BBC television.

1977 *I Read the News Today* is broadcast on BBC Schools Radio.
Daughter Ruth is born.
Liverpool Football Club win the European Cup for the first time

1978 *One for the Road* opens in Liverpool.
Stags and Hens opens at the Everyman Theatre in Liverpool.
The Daughters of Albion is broadcast on television.

1979 Margaret Thatcher leads the right-wing Conservative Party to power. Liverpool, which retains a strong Labour (left-wing) council, often finds itself at odds with the government.

1980 *Educating Rita* is **commissioned** by the Royal Shakespeare Company. It wins the Society of West End Theatre award for Best Comedy.
Daughter Rachel is born.
Riots in Toxteth, close to Liverpool city centre.

1982 A series of plays about working-class Liverpool men, 'Boys from the Blackstuff', is broadcast on BBC television. Written by Alan Bleasdale, who, like Russell, writes mostly about his home city and its people, the plays are hugely popular and well received.

1983 Writes music, lyrics and the book for *Blood Brothers*, which opens in Liverpool, then transfers to London. The show proves to be a massive hit.
Is awarded an honorary MA by the Open University.
Film version of *Educating Rita* opens, starring Michael Caine and Julie Walters. The screenplay is nominated for an Academy Award.

1986 *Shirley Valentine* opens in Liverpool.

1987 Begins writing screenplay for film version of *Shirley Valentine*.

1988 Stage version of *Shirley Valentine* transfers to London.

1989 *Shirley Valentine* wins Olivier Award for Best Comedy of the Year.
Film version of *Shirley Valentine* is made, starring Pauline Collins.
95 Liverpool football fans are crushed to death in the Hillsborough stadium disaster. The resulting inquiry in to what happened at Hillsborough recommended the introduction of all-seater stadia.

1990 Writes *Dancing Thru' the Dark*, a screenplay version of *Stags and Hens*.
Is made a Doctor of Letters by Liverpool University.
Poll tax riots erupt all over Britain, spelling the end for Margaret Thatcher's time as Prime minister.
Margaret Thatcher resigns.

1993 *Terraces* is broadcast by BBC Schools Television.
Blood Brothers opens on Broadway, New York.

1997 A left-wing Labour government, led by Tony Blair, is elected for the first time since 1979.

2000 *The Wrong Boy*, his first novel, is published.

Glossary

adaptation rewriting of a work from its original form into another, e.g. a novel may be adapted into a film script, and the script is then an adaptation

agent someone who works on behalf of artists (usually writers or actors), helping them find work, and encouraging them to produce material

apprentice a young person who signs a contract to learn a trade or craft from an older, experienced worker

aspiration ambition or hope

auditorium area in the interior of a theatre or hall where the audience sits

authoritarian strict

bourgeois term describing something that is associated with the middle class. It is usually used critically, implying that something is pretentious or stuffy.

buoyed supported

busk play an instrument (or sing) on the street to make money from passers-by

charabanc coach or bus

CIA (Central Intelligence Agency) the US intelligence-gathering and spy network. Many politically active students in the 1960s believed that CIA agents were sent out all over the world to report on 'subversive' (anti-government) activity, especially in colleges.

class system system that divides people into groups according to their economic or social position in society

commission (verb) to place an order with an artist, e.g. a theatre asking a writer to write a play especially for that theatre. The work itself is called a commission (noun).

company all the people – actors, designers, director, stage crew – who work together to produce a show in a theatre

critic person who writes reviews of artistic productions (e.g. films, concerts, theatre shows) for newspapers or magazines

demeaned treated with a lack of respect

director person who directs actors in a theatre show or a film, telling them where to move and how to act

disdainful consider someone or something to be inferior

disheartened discouraged or depressed

dormer type of window built into the roof of a house. A dormer bungalow is basically designed as a single-storey dwelling, but it has extra bedrooms in the roof space.

exploit make use of

extended metaphor a metaphor is a writing device where something is described in terms that do not usually apply to it, as if it were something else, e.g. a 'glaring error' does not really glare but it is very noticeable. An extended metaphor is carried on, perhaps through a whole scene or the plot of a play.

farce form of theatrical comedy that relies on comic confusion, multiple exits and entrances and much 'running about'

flagship something that is considered to be a person or organization's most important possession or product

gloss over avoid talking about in detail

Liverpudlian term for someone who comes from or lives in Liverpool

location in films, a place outside the studio where scenes are shot

Luddite person whose thinking is old-fashioned, narrow-minded and backward-looking

manual jobs/labour work done mainly using hands and muscles rather than brain power

materialistic keen on objects and possessions

menagerie varied collection of animals

mental asylum old-fashioned name for a home or hospital for people with psychological problems

meticulous careful and attentive to detail

middle class term for a group of people in society that are thought to exist between the working class and upper class. Sociologists and others have argued for years about what makes a person middle class. No one has come up with a definition and most people today like to think of themselves as middle class, basing this on the sort of job they do and the values they hold.

munitions ammunition (e.g. bullets, shells, bombs)

mythical something that is imaginary or made-up

peripatetic someone who works in more than one place, for example a teacher who works in lots of different schools at the same time

playwright someone who writes plays

production in theatre, the making of a script into a show. The same script can be turned into different styles of production by different directors, actors and companies.

pungent smelly

radical person who holds extreme or revolutionary views (often about politics)

set the scenery built on a theatre stage or in a film studio

shrapnel pieces of bomb or shell casing that splinter and fly out when the shell or bomb explodes

slanging match loud exchange of insults

slums old houses which are poor quality and often run-down

Socialist political and economic movement that aims to introduce a 'classless' society, in which power and wealth will be shared out equally. It is associated with Lenin, the first Communist leader of Russia in the early 20th century.

trades skilled manual jobs, such as plumbing and carpentry

underdog person or team least likely to do well

working class term for people who are usually employed in manual jobs or the trades

Victorian describes something or someone from the period when Queen Victoria was on the throne (1837–1901)

Further reading and sources

Further reading

Most of Willy Russell's plays and film scripts have been published. The following editions have notes that will help you enjoy the plays:

Blood Brothers – Methuen Student Edition (Methuen, 1995)
Educating Rita, Stags and Hens and Blood Brothers: Two plays and a Musical by Willy Russell – Methuen Modern Plays (Methuen, 1986)
Our Day Out (Heinemann Educational, 1993)
Shirley Valentine and One for the Road (Methuen, 1993)

Sources

The main source of information for this book was a long interview between Willy Russell and the author.

Willy Russell and his Plays, John Gill (Countyvise, 1996) contains a long interview with Willy Russell.

At the time of writing there is no biography of Willy Russell available and no websites that contain more information about him and his plays than you will find in the introductions and notes in the books listed in the bibliography.

Websites

Beware of websites that are found by searching using the names of plays. They are often sites set up by amateur theatrical companies to publicize their 'hilarious', 'joyous' productions! For example, there are sites publicizing professional productions and tours of Willy Russell shows. Usually these are linked to theatre ticket booking and information lines.

Index

Titles in the *Creative Lives* series include:

Hardback   0 431 13997 0

Hardback   0 431 13984 9

Hardback   0 431 13994 6

Hardback   0 431 13996 2

Hardback   0 431 13998 9

Hardback   0 431 13995 4

Hardback   0 431 13999 7

Find out about the other titles in this series on our website www.heinemann.co.uk/library